Change|Up

A Guide to Going BIG

P. Nathan Thornberry

1805/2500

Change|Up
A Guide to Going BIG
The Hungry Home Inspector Series
P. Nathan Thornberry

Residential Warranty Services/The Inspector Services Group
698 Pro Med Lane
Carmel, IN 46032

ISBN 978-0-692-28841-2

Cover design by Tiffani Blackburn
Photographs courtesy of ShutterStock.com

Ordering Information:
Quantity sales. Special discounts are available on quantity
purchases by corporations, associations, and others. For
details, contact the publisher at the address above.

Orders by U.S. trade bookstores and wholesalers. Please
contact RWS: Tel: (800) 544-8156; Fax: (877) 307-7056 or
visit inspectorservicesgroup.com

Printed in the United States of America
First Edition September 2014

Table of Contents

If you haven't read The Hungry Home Inspector, you should do that first.

If you like seeing the sequel before the original, carry on!

Sincerely,

P. Nathan Thornberry

Chapter 1
Killer Instinct

One major difference between a "Home Inspector" and a "Home Inspection Business Owner" (or any other type of business owner for that matter) is drive.

There's nothing wrong with living a simple life. It may be the path to happiness and longevity, but it doesn't matter to you if you have the drive that I'm referring to. You could tell a true entrepreneur with this level of drive- this killer instinct- that if they pursue their dream, they will absolutely not live as long a life and it wouldn't matter to them at all. They're going to do it anyhow even if it kills them five years sooner than what they may see as mediocrity.

If this is you, this doesn't mean that you are shallow or reckless, it doesn't mean that you value time with your kids any less or that you don't have a "meaningful life", it is your purpose on this planet and it is a noble one. Your purpose is to give purpose to others and it is a very high calling that comes with immense responsibility. The world will benefit from your ambition and the risks you take that come along with it- whether it be products and services you purchase and the indirect benefit to communities that result, or the very direct positive result on lives you cause by being an employer. From this point forward I will be speaking in terms of "You" because at this point, if you're still reading despite the warning of early death, you're probably going to get more out of this book if we just get straight to the point and put everything in terms of "You."

If you truly have the killer instinct, you will feel less than accepted by someone in your life at some point. You will be made to feel as if you should be ashamed of your ambitions- that you don't realize what is "important in life". When this happens, all you have to do is smile, act nice for about 20 minutes, live at their speed for a moment, then you can go about your world domination after they leave.

You will never be understood by many- you will only be understood by the few.

As you go down the path this book will lead you on, you will have to accept ten basic things. I will put those ten things in the context of your business in each chapter of this book and give you a concise manner in which to apply them to your business;

1. You will never hire yourself (and you don't want to).

2. You are always in the way.

3. Time is your enemy.

4. The shorter your outlook, the less successful you will be.

5. Your fees are not what you are worth.

6. Working is a losing proposition.

7. The customer is never right.

8. When in doubt, write a check.

9. What's in your bank account doesn't matter.

10. Debt doesn't matter.

It may seem strange in a book designed to take you from $50,000.00 or $250,000.00 per year in sales up to the $500,000.00 or $1,000,000.00 to say things like "What's in your bank account doesn't matter," but it's true. Truly success-driven people don't talk about how much gold they have in a safe or how many acres they own. They don't speak of how they are debt free. Truly success-driven people think in terms of what their gross sales are or how many competitors they have taken over in the marketplace. When they talk about money, it is usually in terms of how they've blown it on fun things like big boats, cool cars, and ridiculous vacations.

Paying off your mortgage is not a goal you want to have. Bringing in enough money to pay the mortgage on 6 luxury homes in 4 different countries is the goal you want to have. That's not to say you will buy 6 homes, it's more of a mindset issue. Being able to do it or having the goal of doing it is much more appealing than simply paying off your mortgage and being debt free.

Here is the reality of home inspection;

It's an extremely specialized skill, requiring general knowledge of many systems. It requires the ability to take the information in front of you and deliver it in a concise manner. It's also not the most profitable business you can be in. If you want to make a lot of money easily, there are ways to do it. You could start a restoration company and make obscene money off of insurance claims, but you didn't...because home inspection interests you.

Beyond Insurance Restoration, there are a thousand other businesses in which to make money. At some point you may diversify, but if you are reading this book, you probably already have a background in inspection. As a result, for the time being at least, your quickest method of achieving even more success is likely in growing that home inspection business.

Answer the following question, honestly, to yourself;

Would you rather...

a. Do a home inspection for $300.00.

b. Do a home inspection for $500.00.

c. Do a mold test for $300.00.

If your answer was "a", you are probably guessing at where I'm going with the rules above- specifically #5 (Your fees are not what you are worth). If you answered "b", you are probably approaching this from a mathematical standpoint, which is in many ways prudent. If you answered "c", you are not only approaching the question from a mathematical standpoint but you are also accounting for your time. Kudos. *Now go sign up at www.InspectorLab.com!*

If you did not find an answer which felt like the right one, you are on the right track. Ultimately, the correct answer from a business perspective is "none of the above".

We will delve into why that is the correct answer later on in this book. If you love inspecting homes, you should absolutely be inspecting homes (especially if you're good at it). If it fascinates you every day, you love dealing with clients, and you love finding defects which others may have missed... you are in the right business my friend! You may just not have the right position in that business for optimal growth. First and foremost, you are an owner. It does not necessarily mean you are the marketing guy, the web designer, the general manager, the lead inspector, or the bookkeeper. I realize it is un-American (and un-Canadian) to deface a book, but I invite you to write in this one on the chart below. If you want a new copy of this book after you're done send me a note, I'll sign it inside the front cover and even pay the shipping. Just hop on www.homeinspectionforum.net and let me know in the member's only area that you finished the book...I'll ship it out to you right away! Alternatively, you can make a chart on another piece of paper...but do it with a pen rather than a mouse. It's much more meaningful when you write things down.

My Position(s) in the Home Inspection Business

Position

    Strength/Weakness   Love it/Like it/Hate it

Booking Inspections

_____   _____

Inspecting

_____   _____

Report Writing

_____   _____

Managing Inspectors

_____   _____

Hiring Inspectors

_____   _____

Handling Complaints

_____   _____

Managing the Office

_____   _____

Hiring Office Personnel

_____   _____

Bookkeeping

_____   _____

Web Development

_____   _____

Marketing

_____   _____

Sales

_____   _____

Let's say you were working at the head offices of a major corporation. One with not just $1 million in sales or $10 million in sales, but more like $1 billion or more in sales. Your position is CEO, and on your floor of the building you have one or more people working almost directly with you on a day to day basis performing each of the tasks listed above, with the exception of the inspection-specific stuff of course.

If you had someone doing sales who was not really good at it and didn't love it either, how long would it take you to fire them?

The best CEOs in the world make these decisions very quickly and spend big money making sure they have the right people in the right positions to start. They also tend to be physically fit (or at least try), read a lot (which you are in the process of doing), wake up early, and eat/drink right.

Today, declare yourself CEO of your Inspection Company. This is definitely the easiest of the tasks I am going to give you in this book, but probably the most meaningful.

Chapter 2
I'm Fired

There are two reasons you wish there were more of you. The first is you have simply devalued yourself into a labor intensive process and you need slave labor that you don't have to train. The second is you have bitten off more than you can chew and you want a vacation sometime in the next 20 years. There are plenty of other useful purposes a clone could serve. Magic tricks, alibis, spare parts- the list is endless.

There is one thing a clone should never be- an employee.

In Chapter One I gave you a chart in which to fill. Here is mine:

My Position(s) in My Business

Position

	Strength/Weakness	**Love it/Like it/Hate it**
Taking Orders		
	Neutral	*Neutral*
Legal Issues		
	Strength	*Hate it*

Managing Sales Force
  Weakness   *Neutral*

Handling Complaints
  Strength   *Hate it*

Managing the Office
  Weakness   *Hate it*

Hiring Personnel
  Weakness   *Like it*

Bookkeeping
  Weakness   *Hate it*

Product Development
  Strength   *Love it*

Web Development
  Weakness   *Hate it*

Marketing
  Strength   *Love it*

Sales
  Strength   *Hate it*

Design
  Weakness   *Love it*

I had to adjust the categories a bit, but this is essentially the same chart I gave you. After I filled this out (years ago with a consultant), I realized what a lousy employee I truly am, and why I have been fired so many times.

Here is my real quick analysis in one paragraph:

When the phone rings it's usually an order, which I absolutely can do but I don't have the time or the patience. I don't know how anyone can love it, but I have half a dozen people who do it all day with smiles on their faces. Legal issues I have always been great at, and there are parts of it I love, but the mental anguish of dealing with the negativity makes me hate it. When I manage my sales force, I am great at setting goals, but my personal ability to pay attention to the detail of reporting daily makes it my weakness. I can handle a complaint like nobody's business and turn the biggest complainer into a raving fan...but once again the negativity of the situation makes it so I could not do that every day and love my job. Managing the office is a major weakness- I ordered toilet paper once online and instead of putting the number of boxes desired I put the number of rolls and now we have a virtually endless supply of toilet paper in the office- we are actually encouraging employees to steal it. I am good at reading people, but when it comes to hiring, I am an optimist and have found I will hire someone to give them a chance much too often. Bookkeeping is a big fat no. Product development has made my career and is my calling. Web development is a non-starter for me. I have never learned how to do web development from a technical standpoint- but I can tell you exactly what needs to be on the web page and am great at the marketing side of things. Sales is a skill. I have it, but I hate it. I hate being sold to, and therefore I hate selling. I cannot draw to save my life, but I love creating.

Perhaps after you read my admissions of being terrible at some of the things I love to do, hating other things that I do very well, and having really only a couple of things I not only excel at but also enjoy doing, it will have you going back to Chapter 1 to make some adjustments. You cannot just love one part of a category- you have to love all aspects of it, and there is nothing wrong with admitting your weaknesses.

Weaknesses do not necessarily mean you are not good at something if you really apply yourself. I am certain if I locked myself in our accounting department and did nothing but write checks all day, I could do it accurately, I just can't do it effectively when my mind is in other places.

At the end of the day, I am a marketer and product development guy. Anything else I do in my business is a bad use of my time and probably doesn't deliver the best possible outcome for my business or my clients.

Perhaps you are an expert bookkeeper and inspector, and you love doing both. Maybe you're great at managing people but not so great at hiring them.

Some of the most successful inspectors I know are true inspectors through and through. They love going to homes and inspecting them. They also usually have one other skill set- and that would be the product development side of things (marketing). Everything else on the list is either a weakness or they hate it, so they hire others to perform those tasks or they outsource them.

I don't know any home inspector who built his/her own

website and does over $1 million a year. I only know of one who actually does sales. I am not familiar with any who answers all company phone calls. Not one of them ever hired someone just like them. They all looked for staff with different skill sets- people who could fill the void left by their weaknesses and the things they didn't like to do.

It may seem easy to afford the luxury of not having to answer phones or build websites or anything else on the list that isn't your forte if you are bringing in seven figures, and a difficulty if you're bringing in five figures. It seems this way because it is definitely true, but I'm not telling you to hire a bunch of people tomorrow. It would be next to impossible for most home inspection business owners without a winning lottery ticket in their hands.

What you need to do now is go back to the list again. Here is a fresh copy;

My Position(s) in the Home Inspection Business

Position

> **Strength/Weakness   Love it/Like it/Hate it**
> **Rank (1-12)**

Booking Inspections

_____   _____

_____

Inspecting

_____   _____

_____

Report Writing

_____   _____

_____

Managing Inspectors

_____   _____

_____

Hiring Inspectors

_____   _____

_____

Handling Complaints

_____   _____

_____

Managing the Office

_____   _____

_____

Hiring Office Personnel

_____   _____

_____

Bookkeeping

_____   _____

_____

Web Development

_____   _____

_____

Marketing

_____   _____

_____

Sales

_____   _____

_____

This time you'll notice a new column- "Rank". In this column, I want you to rank the Strengths you have that you also Like/Love in the order in which you enjoy them most. Then continue down the rankings to number 12 being something that you not only hate, but is also a weakness. *Your worst category*.

As you analyze this chart for yourself, I think you will discover that not only would hiring another "you" be disastrous for your business, but you probably need to fire yourself from multiple positions you hold at your own company. This is not a move you need to make to feel better or be happier. This is not that kind of book. This is a move you need to make for the success of your home inspection business and for the future of every employee, vendor, and supplier who may benefit from the economic impact you will have on the world.

So let's focus on just that worst category. Number 12.

What you need to do right now is get it off your plate-no matter what it is. If it's Sales, hire a part time sales person. It doesn't have to cost much to have someone deliver brochures and talk you up in real estate offices one day a week (which is probably more than you're doing right now if you hate it). If it's marketing, hire a local firm or go to www.ultimateinspectormarketing.com and just sub it out. Hire a bookkeeper, outsource your phone answering...pretty much anything on the list has an immediately available and effective solution.

I'm not kidding. Put the book down, research a

solution to a problem, and implement it. It doesn't matter how well (or how poorly) you implement it, you can always make adjustments later. If you're going to get to seven figures in your business, you're going to have to learn very quickly that "doing" is much more important than doing something perfectly.

Chapter 3
Move (Get Out the Way)

It's generally a bad idea to hire cocaine users, but sometimes it pays off, as it did for me in 2006. At the age of 24, I had not only the home warranty business (including the 90-Day Warranties for home inspectors), but I also dabbled in construction and home repair, which in hindsight I realize is a genetic disorder. At one point I had multiple HVAC trucks, appliance repair trucks, remodeling crews, and the smallest division...roofing. It was the one area I was least comfortable with, but one day in 2003 (three years earlier) I had a roofer walk in my door looking for a job. He was presentable, well spoken, very upbeat (later turned out that was the cocaine) and was ready to work basically on commission. I thought "sure, why not."

I bought him a truck, gave him the ability to buy on our accounts, and he went to work doing mostly leak repairs.

About two months after he started working for me, he came by the office with a check for $24,000.00 (which translates to about $1 million to a 21 year old) and told me it was just a deposit on a roof replacement job. We sat down, went through his estimates, ordered materials, and sure enough he completed, with the help of an assistant, a roof installation for 3 buildings at a pork farm.

The profit from this job was over $10,000.00.

As you can imagine, I was interested in getting more of these roof replacement jobs. I asked him how he got it, and basically he said it wasn't anything more than a referral.

Just then, in his cocaine-induced excitement, he made a suggestion to me that would change everything. He said we needed a yellow pages ad.

I called the phone book company and they actually sent a rep out to meet me. I negotiated with them for an hour until I finally got something I could live with- $600.00 a month for the very first ad in the roofing section, a full color business card size ad essentially within the column. (Most of the larger companies had one or two page spreads on the following pages)

The business from that was okay, but a couple of years later the drug use issues of this employee became apparent and I had to let him go. Luckily, I had a couple of good general contractors on the payroll who knew how to sub out roof installs, so we made the most out of the calls we were getting off of the ads, but we planned on discontinuing them.

Then hail came to Indianapolis in a big way in 2006.

I'm not sure of the exact number, but I'd say half of the homes in Indianapolis had roof claims. Our phones were ringing off the hook. We went from 4 estimates a week to over 50 calls an hour- not from people thinking about maybe replacing their roof but people who needed one immediately and virtually had an insurance check in hand.

The marketing was a success, mostly dumb luck stemming from the advice of a cocaine addict, but the execution left much to be desired. I had not built the business for 400 calls a day, much less 400 calls that required estimates and insurance paperwork with which I was not familiar.

So I did the most foolish thing I could do. I started giving the calls to my job supervisors and even running them myself. We were running 10 hour days and speeding from house to house trying to keep up with demand and not even closing most of the jobs...they were just taking our estimates, getting checks from their insurers, and finding a cheaper provider.

I was in the way.

Eventually I got smart, hired an outside group to manage the process, and within 24 hours of signing a contract with them, we opened a new warehouse. We had shipments of shingles coming in and real contracts to go out with our estimates, 15 professional estimators, a fully staffed billing department, a supervisor, and just over 30 crews to install.

This probably cut my potential profit on any individual job by 60%, which may sound steep, but I literally had to do nothing else for two years thereafter with my roofing division and we did millions (over $6 million per year) in roofing and siding alone. The only effort I had to make was opening an envelope every week with my check in it.

This is about the most extreme example I can think of from my own personal experiences of being in the way as an owner. Actually, it's an example of both not being in the way and being in the way at the same time. Ironically, the smartest thing I ever did in that business was take the advice of a drug addict. I got out of the way, trusted the advice, and let one of my employees be empowered in making a decision as to where we should advertise a line of business- almost as a reward for having brought in a single job with a $10,000.00 profit margin.

The dumbest thing I did was listen to myself, and try to take on these bids - and then I got out of the way again and let the professionals take over. I had done my part, and that was the marketing and branding that made us one of the top roofing companies in the market by volume. Oftentimes inspectors tell me they do not hire because they cannot find the right person. I found a cocaine user and the hire resulted in seven-figure revenue. I am sure you can do even better!

Sometimes being in the way isn't so obvious or extreme. Sometimes it's sitting quietly right in front of you on your desk.

The indisputable #1 reason home inspectors stand in the way of their own business growth is in their report. It's a touchy subject for most- I've probably reviewed 200+ reports for inspectors and every single time I feel like I'm calling their baby ugly.

Here's a really simple solution for you: Find the most successful inspection company you can- one with 10+ inspectors, preferably in a huge market where there are over a hundred companies. Lie, cheat, steal (or just ask them) for a sample report. You might even find one on their website.

Swipe and Deploy.

Do not get caught up in details. Do not start comparing your report to theirs and saying "mine is better because of..." or look at the number of photos you have and say "I always take a picture of X in order to avoid that question or liability...". None of these things you're saying about the report are very credible unless you have more inspectors than they, and have higher gross revenue. If you don't, you're wrong, plain and simple. You are staring success in the face, and standing in the way.

Let's apply this to another industry in order to take the emotion out of it. Let's say there are two bars in your town- both similarly located and with nice interiors. Everything about these two bars is virtually the same with one glaring exception- one bar has over twenty beers on tap and the other has none. The bar with twenty beers on tap does $3 million a year, the bar with none does $250,000.00 per year.

Before I go any further, if I were to tell you that the bar owner who does $250,000.00 per year has a really, really good reason why he doesn't have beer on tap, would you care?

Here, I'll give you the reasons. The first reason he had was that installing the tap system, including the refrigeration down the lines, was expensive. The second reason is that he didn't want the liability of his bartenders pouring the beer into a potentially contaminated glass when there is a zero liability option in bottles. The glasses would have to be cleaned as well and he would need to buy more of them. The third reason is that people can get sick off beer, and sue the bar, if a single keg goes more than 4 months without being changed out- and by the way, when it gets changed out, you lose whatever product is in the bottom of that keg.

So this bar owner's really good reasons for doing less than 10% of the revenue of the guy down the street and driving a Buick LeSabre instead of a Lamborghini Gallardo, is liability, upfront costs, and potential losses of product. I am not a beer drinker. I have not once finished a single beer in all of my life, but if I started a bar tomorrow I'd have more taps than anyone else in town.

If I were to tell that same failing bar owner that your report was 10 pages longer than it had to be, had unnecessary narratives and pictures, and lacked some of the features of more profitable inspection companies that do ten times the revenue because of the fear of liability, expense, and wanting to avoid questions that come up every now and then from buyers, even he would know it was a foolish mistake.

It's easy for all of us to see the mistakes others make, but we are largely blind to our own. Perhaps your report doesn't need revamping, it may be perfectly fine. One thing is for certain- if you are doing less than $1 million per year in the home inspection business, there is something you're not doing right.

What is the difference between you and the owner of the $1 million + home inspection business down the street or in the next State? I promise they are not smarter than you, they are not a "better inspector", they are not an MBA from Harvard...they have just moved out of the way.

Now is the time to pick three aspects of your business in which you are in the way and fix it. I have had to do this as well, and it's not always easy!

Once you've picked your three, go to www.homeinspectionforum.net, register, and post in the member's only discussion section what your three ways are. Successful home inspection business owners from all over the U.S. and Canada will give you feedback that could save you weeks of aggravation.

Chapter 4
Time Is Your Enemy

Aggravation behind the wheel of a car or truck- more commonly known as "Road Rage"- is completely misunderstood. Many people believe that it's caused by traffic jams on roads like Interstate 10 in Los Angeles, where an extra hour or two driving to get back to your home in the valley from work is commonplace. Other people believe it stems from reactions to the bad driving of others. Some believe that this rage is just caused by angry people behind the wheel.

They're all mistaken.

The cause is the differences in speed at which people live. It's not even a theory, it's a fact, and if you disagree feel free to write your own book. It seems to me there are many people in the world who believe they are immortal, ironically when they are most at risk of dying (behind the wheel). I am not so naïve, I realize fully that my time on this earth is limited and whether I want to spend my time with my kids, getting through a project, or riding roller coasters…I'm going to do that and no one can get in my way. (Except when they're behind the wheel of the other car)

"Nine you're fine, ten you're mine" is the rule by which most police officers live. That means if the speed limit is 35 MPH, go 44 and you probably won't run into trouble. Tap your brakes if you roll by an officer and they will feel as if you were intimidated by their authority and you won't likely get pulled over. If you have a very open road, no cops for miles and clear visibility...take a risk. The ROI is pretty good. Don't be stupid or dangerous about it, but if we're honest with each other I think we will agree that neither of us have ever owned a car that didn't hit 90 MPH at one point or another on an Interstate.

Sure, you'll probably get pulled over at one point or another. It's happened to me 37 times as I write this book with a total of six citations issued and one that held up and had to be paid. I would have gotten out of that one if I were not a minor at the time, as it was an extreme disadvantage not being able to represent myself in the proceedings. I had prepared everything I needed, and had proof that the owner of the vehicle I was operating (Patty Thornberry) had negligently installed tires of the wrong size on the custom van in which I was issued the citation.

Drive a Porsche every day of the year except one and I get a ticket. In a mom van...unbelievable.

Whether it's people who go 2 MPH under the speed limit on two lane roads, people taking up the whole moving walkway at the airport and not even walking but standing, or the cashier at the gas station having a full out conversation about the lottery with the patron in front of you, time vampires are everywhere and it should make you angry. You have business to take care of.

Here's a big secret about very driven entrepreneurs: They care more than anyone about other people.

It may not seem like it to most, but it's true. We know that the more we accomplish, the more we can truly help people in our communities and our checkbooks can oftentimes speak louder than actions or words. Even if you do not outright pay money to a charitable organization (which they oftentimes need more than donation of your time or used household goods), you will make a huge impact on your community by creating jobs and encouraging economic activity.

You may come off as less than personable at times. You may get easily agitated by the slow driver in front of you and show your frustration, but it's for best. You cannot allow the slow or unlucky to get in your way, and by "unlucky" I mean people who constantly have problems in their lives. Maybe they constantly have money problems. Maybe they have relationship issues, or perhaps they just complain a lot about life. You are not being insensitive by ignoring them. You have to ignore them for your own sanity and productivity. In the time it takes you to console one person about their issues in futility, you can change the lives of many others in a meaningful way.

This applies not only to your personal life, but also to your business.

Whether it is a vendor, an employee, a client, or another inspector...avoid negativity and time vampires. Avoid the unlucky, and those who need your help in such a way that it will take away from your ability to help others who deserve it.

I had an employee once, we'll call him "Dominic", just to keep it anonymous. I hired him as a call center employee, and this was back when I was personally interviewing everyone who got hired. He came to the interview prepared- clean cut, well dressed, even had a binder with a project he had done with spreadsheets and reports. He spoke well at the interview.

He had pages and pages of documents you'd have to be an expert computer user to be able to put together, his communication skills were excellent and ambition was there. I hired him on the spot.

Huge mistake.

I'm not sure I could have avoided making that mistake, but from that point forward I made a mistake every single day I kept him on board.

First he couldn't book an inspection to save his life. Then he started getting very nervous, and his communication skills diminished. I moved him to a simpler position, just reception duties. When he couldn't handle that, I created a job out of thin air for him, delivering lunch to employees at their desks.

He was a great guy, and I wanted to help him. It ended up costing me time and money. Once he started falling off step stools in the kitchen and breaking things, he pretty much needed to go because he was now a liability on top of everything else...but I still kept him.

The worst part- I never let him go. He ended up getting a job offer for double what he was being paid at my office from someone in the same industry, probably because they thought if I had him on board he was incredibly valuable.

Maybe he was incredibly valuable. Maybe it was my failure in exploiting that value and ultimately not being able to give him advancement opportunities. Either way, as it turns out, he was going to be just fine after he left.

People who are willing to put in the effort, who work hard, will find a way. People who don't want to take care of themselves won't. Be fearless in letting anyone go, and be determined to keep anyone around who has value. Someone in your business delivering value will continue to do so. Someone in your business delivering negative value will continue to do so, and they must be disposed of immediately.

Take it from someone who has literally spent hundreds of thousands of dollars on problematic people...they never get any better. There are very few correctable mistakes or behaviors. I have never had one employee who was late to work several times, made spelling and grammatical errors over and over, cause more than one issue in customer service, or any other bad behavior, who ever corrected it. Ever. They all eventually end up being fired or quitting.

Whether someone is driving a car in front of you at 10 MPH under the speed limit, or working unproductively in your business, they are both the same kind of problem. The difference is the latter is within your control.

In order to turn the tables and make time your friend, you have to deploy solutions that not only make your time more valuable, but ultimately make time a non-issue.

Start with the simple step of outsourcing anything you can afford to immediately, both in your business and your personal life. Mowing the lawn and shoveling snow off the driveway should be first on the list. Cleaning the house should be next.

Do not change your own oil. Do not wash your own car.

I've maybe added $200.00 a month to your expenses on the high end, probably more like $100.00, but add up the hours:

Mowing 3 times per month:	3 hours
Cleaning:	3 hours
Changing your own oil:	1 hour
Hand washing a car:	1 hour

That's 8 hours, for a total of $12.50 per hour to $25.00 per hour on the high side.

Here's a pretty easy question for you:

If you could actually hire a person with not only your knowledge and skill set, but also your exact level of decision making capability, ambition, and ability to communicate, would you be willing to pay that person $12.50 to $25.00 per hour?

The obvious answer is "yes", and therefore the list above is a no-brainer. Do the same for fertilizing, landscaping, painting, and repairs around the house. Also outsource anything where there is a reasonably priced alternative to doing something yourself, and never work for hours to save $100.00 on anything.

You don't even have to be open to hiring employees if that's something you are averse to in order to take advantage of outsourcing these types of services. In fact, this is a great way to reduce the number of staff members you will ultimately need regardless of your goals and will make your operation much more efficient.

Now let's look at other services you can outsource, specific to the home inspection industry.

1.   **Sending out confirmation emails/communications with clients**

    a.   Never do this. It's a nominal fee from a system like ISN (Inspection Support Network).

2.   **Taking phone calls and booking inspections.**

    a.   No excuse to do this, unless you feel you are personally worth around $12.00 an hour. It's a nominal fee from call centers like the ISG Call Center.

3.   **Taking complaints.**

a.   Some of them you may have to handle, but you can take 75% of them off your plate when you offer a warranty. Unless there is a big issue or a marketing opportunity involved, it's not worth your time or negative energy.

These are just three simple personal and business processes which take no more than a few hours to set up and you get the benefit of hours and hours saved monthly for the rest of your career. Get rid of mowing, cleaning and dealing with automotive needs on the personal side. Then ditch the administrative work associated with booking an inspection. Do not take the call in the first place, and outsource your complaint handling in an effective way.

You are in a position to do all of the above- whether you are just starting out or are an experienced inspector doing six figures. If you are driven, you will do it. It is not a sales pitch, I have no financial interest in ISN. There is pretty much one other call center in the industry, so interview both before moving forward on that topic. If you put the warranty issue aside for the moment, that is unfortunate, but probably the least damaging to your business from a time management perspective (and probably the most damaging from a marketing perspective).

Later we will get into more areas you should outsource and staff, but right now you need to take action. CEO's make decisions quickly and they act fast.

I think it is about time you called a lawn mowing company.

Chapter 5
The Shorter Your Outlook, The Less Successful You Will Be.

Facebook Sucks.

This is the first line of a hilarious presentation I have done on Social Media to Home Inspectors and Real Estate Agents throughout the U.S. and Canada (see more at www.Nathan.tv), but I don't really mean that Facebook sucks. Facebook won the game in the Social Media space, mostly by offering nearly every feature for free.

Facebook is a great example of being wildly successful by having a very long outlook. Facebook is headed for $10 Billion in revenue...and it all started with "free".

Those starting businesses for the first time today, especially younger people, are lucky to have Facebook and other dot com's as a model. The world went from "here's my product, buy it", to "here's someone else's product (ads), buy it", to "here's information (Google) and all of your friends (Facebook), so just live here all day and eventually somebody is going to buy or sell something."

Ignoring this phenomenon in your service business (home inspection) is a mistake.

Look at the models we see even in our industry. The two most successful vendors (and yes, Associations are vendors) are The Inspector Services Group (RecallChek, 90-Day Warranties, InspectorLab, etc.) and InterNACHI (Certified Master Inspector, Inspector Outlet, etc.). There are literally two entities within the home inspection industry which have ever come close to (and exceeded) the 8-figure mark...why do you think that is?

It's all about outlook.

I would estimate that between Nick and myself we have probably given away over $5 million in memberships and products just in the last 5 years alone. It wasn't that we were stupid or frivolous, it was that we both knew what we had was good. We had something clients would likely continue utilizing, and we were both looking 5 and 10 years down the line.

We even did a nationwide tour with 40+ stops to actually meet inspectors, give a four hour presentation, and hand them free stuff. My expense just for being there was in the six figures. Add the giveaways and we are looking at around the $500,000.00 mark. I imagine Nick spent more than that.

This was quite the departure from where I was and what I was doing 10 years prior. Back then, I had zero outlook. I was concerned about what I was going to sell next week and the week after, perhaps tricking myself into thinking that what I was doing was right because I looked at last years numbers and I was up 30%-40% in home warranty sales.

Looking at your numbers today compared to last year is NOT the same as having a long outlook. It's the opposite.

Back then I was hindered by two major business disabilities which kept me from getting where I really wanted to be:

1. **The perception that cash next week was important.**

2. **The perception that making the sale was a good thing.**

The perception that cash next week, next month, or even the next day being important was a tough one to break. We all need cash to run our businesses and pay the bills, but don't make the mistake I did. It took me until the point where I was doing moderately well to drop that perception- but later it proved to be nothing more than a mindset issue.

I say it was "proved" because years later, during one of the worst times in real estate (2008-2009), my cash flow was impacted in a significant way- and when I say in a significant way I mean in a devastating way. I went from a very comfortable six figures in the bank at all times to one of the darkest winters ever. It was definitely a credit card Christmas, and there were months where I didn't know if I'd be able to maintain appropriate reserves.

While it was stressful, and I did what I had to do, I had already learned the value of having a long outlook. It became clear that years earlier the stress of looking for immediate cash flow was largely unproductive. You spend 100% of your mental energy on it while you're only effective at dealing with it maybe half the time (and probably less). When you are not directly involved in making sales happen, when you go home and you're having dinner with your family, you still have the stress even though there is nothing you can do about it at that moment. When you're sitting at your desk in your home office at 9:00, the kids have gone to bed, and there is nothing you can possibly do to make cash happen at that moment, you still stress about it!

This prevents you from truly working on your business. It keeps you from having that long outlook needed to make business happen.

The solution is simple: Only think about money at the exact moments when you can do something about it. All of the other moments should be spent thinking about and implementing future success exclusively (and forget about your current cash flow issues).

To put this in terms of your business, your hours are very likely 8:00 AM to 5:30 PM or something close to it. You're either starting an inspection at 8:00 AM or you're on the phone booking an inspection for the next day. By 10:00 AM if you're not on an inspection, hopefully you are stopping by real estate offices and dropping off brochures, or prospecting. The cash flow you need to make happen is what you do from 8:00 AM to 5:30 PM. That's when most of your clients want you to inspect. That is when the real estate offices are open, and those are the hours in which you're going to get most of your phone calls. Take no prisoners during that time. When you're on an inspection or taking an order, forget about all of your stresses and gamify the process- to win the game, you have to upsell, deliver great service, create ongoing referrals, and protect your assets.

When 5:30 PM hits, your workday is over.

Now is the time to work on your business and have an outlook much further out than your competition. Start with taking that time to add additional services to your business- Mold Testing, Pool Inspections, Radon Testing, etc. Next start writing personal notes to agents you are targeting for business. Then start examining the competition and evaluate the marketplace- figure out from numbers published by local REALTOR boards how many residential transactions there are annually, research who the largest offices are in town and who the best-selling agents are. You must know who your competition is and what they offer, and use that information to further develop your product and pricing.

Now you're going to have a good day every day. You spend 8:00 AM to 5:30 PM playing a game, and you spend 5:30 PM to 11:00 PM innovating and creating a great business model. Over time, money will become a non-issue totally, and you will find that any time worrying about money or current cash flow is an absolute waste.

Chapter 6
Your Fees Are Not What
You Are Worth

One of the worst pieces of advice you will hear from anyone in any business is "raise your prices".

It's not bad advice on its face. After all, it doesn't take a genius to figure out that if you charge more for a product or service then your margins on an individual sale are higher if you raise your prices. It is bad advice because it isn't qualified advice.

In Chapter 1 I suggested to you that there were thousands of businesses more profitable than home inspection, and one of those is most certainly being a consultant. Here is a basic guide to becoming a consultant:

1. Call yourself a consultant. Buy business cards.

2. Make a resume for yourself that sounds really, really good.

3. Charge a fee for your consultation services.

4. Tell your clients to raise their prices.

It's a ridiculously simple business model, but it has worked literally hundreds of thousands of times. Just tell clients they'll be driving a Lamborghini in no time, and have "real clients" sit in a chair outside with a yacht behind them singing your praises. That will get the job done. Do not forget to put "results not typical" in the fine print at the bottom of the screen.

Both you and I have no interest in being in that space, We probably both have too much integrity for it, but at some point or another you're either going to receive (or have the inclination to give) this advice from someone even worse than a paid consultant...it's going to come from an unpaid consultant.

Maybe it's a competitor looking to "help you out." Maybe it's an inspector half way across the country on a message board delivering the message...either way it's unqualified advice.

Why is it that especially in the service industry there is such an emphasis on raising prices without any justification?

The simple answer is ego.

If currency is a measure of trade value, then the more currency you receive as a direct result of your chosen profession for a single event, the more valuable you feel you are. At least on a micro-economic level this rings true.

To a certain extent, the "my fee for an inspection is really high" inspector is valuing himself in terms of a loaf of bread. If a loaf of bread costs $3.00, and he charges $600.00 for a home inspection, then it stands to reason that a baker in the colonial town where this inspectors mindset is two hundred years ago would have to slave over an oven for a whole day or two pumping out 200 loaves of bread in exchange for his home inspection brilliance in a single appointment.

On an even more basic level than ego, this mindset is one from childhood that one never grew out of. At least until the dot com era, being a doctor or a lawyer was definitely something which symbolized respect in the community, high education levels, and financial stability. We've probably all heard of parents wanting their kids to become a doctor or a lawyer. Many inspectors (and other service providers) thinking in the mindset of how much can they charge for a single event, are essentially clinging to an infantile desire to make their parents proud.

There is nothing wrong with that necessarily. It can make for a good living. I'm sure they have made their parents proud, too.

The problem with this mindset is it has never once, in the history of home inspection, led to a $1 million + home inspection business...ever. The most it has probably ever resulted in is around a $250,000.00 business- which again, is quite respectable, but if you are reading this book you probably want more.

In order for you to reach your maximum value, you have to detach that value from your fees. What you make on an individual inspection event is inconsequential. What you make annually is what matters. Would you rather make (net) $1,000,000.00 a year, and lose money on half of your inspections booked, or make $999,999.00 and make money on every single deal? The correct answer for someone who wants to make a million bucks is obvious. But if your ego stands in the way and you have to make money on every single deal in order to feel good about yourself- you've broken every concept in this book at once! (You should definitely fire yourself as your accountant. You are definitely in the way, even thinking that way is a waste of time. Your outlook is about as far as the tip of your nose, and for crying out loud your fees are not what you're worth!)

Now let's assume you picked the first answer, and are willing to make as much money or as little money (or even lose money) on any given transaction in order to aim for the larger targets of Gross Revenue and Net Profit.

Now you need to revisit that research you started doing at the end of Chapter 4. What were your competitors charging for a 1500 square foot home inspection? How many inspectors are there in your market? How many residential real estate transactions occurred?

It would be impossible for me to give the correct answer for every possible combination of the answers above for every market in the U.S. and Canada, so I'm going to give you some sample numbers and you can figure out what you need to do in your market from there.

Let's say you did your market research and your competition ranged from $175.00 to $475.00 on a 1500 square foot base inspection, but 80% of the competition was in the $250.00-$350.00 range.

Let us also assume you are not at your target volume. We can say you have aspirations of being a 10 man inspection firm and doing 5,000 full inspections annually.

The first assumption you have to make is that you will never exceed 20-25% of the market for home inspections locally. This has been the case in nearly every major market in the U.S. and Canada. So if you've found that local real estate transactions number less than 20,000-25,000 units annually, you need to back up and look at reasonable expansion markets within a 1-2 hour drive. Otherwise you need to back off of your 5,000 inspection goal and look into the number of inspectors that will be necessary.

Assuming you have the market space for the 5,000 inspections, and your competition is largely in the $250.00-$350.00 range, then you need to determine if you are at or below 80% of your target volume.

In home inspection, volume comes before price. Once an agent uses your services, they are very likely to return again, but getting them to you in the first place is about two things:

1. Overcoming objections you can control (mainly price)

2. Giving the benefits that can drive them to switch (i.e. 90-Day Warranties, SewerGard, RecallChek, etc.)

Of course you have to exude professionalism regardless of whether you have the best price and the most differentiators in the marketplace.

So let's assume you are at or below 80% of your target volume and looking to increase your volume. Your price, in this scenario, should start at around $225.00.

It may sound crazy, but it's not I assure you! This price is something that you can put on the front of your professionally printed brochures... "Inspections Starting at Only $225.00!"

In reality, this is a starting price, and I would go up to 1000 square feet with it, then have price increases at 500 square foot intervals all the way up to 5000 square feet. I would then jump by 1000 at a time- but at the higher square footages you can be right in line with the median competitors. If you want to make your pricing model very complex and have additional charges for age, crawl spaces, or extra drive time, you will absolutely stunt your growth.

Here's the other key- you need to have a big menu, something you've been building ever since you started working at night on your business as suggested in Chapter 4.

The result you are looking for here is to have one of the lowest reasonable entry-level prices for home inspections and obliterate any potential market objections to giving your services a try. At the same time you are delivering one-stop shopping and enough add-on services that your average ticket is toward the high end of the marketplace and establish a volume level that allows you to continue to invest in a more diverse menu and better equipment and resources.

Now you are creating systems, and I am not just referring to the way in which a service is completed, I am referring to money making systems which can be replicated.

Chapter 7
Working is a Losing Proposition

Break time at Rockefeller Center (circa 1932) is about the best representation of what working is all about- dying. Granted, fatalities on the site were rare as far as we know, the picture is almost certainly staged and situated directly above a solid surface, but I don't see anyone with the last name Rockefeller there either. He was safely somewhere else.

John D. Rockefeller was the first American Billionaire- and adjusted for inflation, probably the richest man ever. We can have a debate regarding his contributions to modern America (and the world), find many faults with the man and his many positives including in the area of philanthropy, but at the end of it all we can both agree that he would not have gone as far in life if he were anywhere near Rockefeller Center during its construction. (As in, actually performing construction duties and putting in a good day's work!)

This may very well be the most controversial chapter in this book, and it will no doubt draw criticism, but I'm going to be very direct when I say to you that working is the worst possible thing you can do for your company. There's nothing good about the act of actually working, and nearly everybody who is doing it right now has the ultimate goal of never doing it again at some point (retirement).

Think about that for a second. For all the blue collar tenacity in our industry, the immediate dismissal of anyone not personally crawling in crawl spaces every day as someone who can't offer real advice, the chest pounding, and all the other nonsense...every single one of them has marked on their calendar a day when they go on permanent fishing vacation.

In contrast, you have the most successful guy in home inspection, Chad Hett (Co-owner of The Elite Group), who has never inspected a home (and never will) yet he just continues to grow his business while ignoring the advice of anyone who has been in a crawl space in the last year or two. You have Alan Carson, who could have retired decades ago (not saying he's old!), but continues to take his company Carson Dunlop to new heights year after year.

Neither have a retirement day on their calendar.

I don't think it is coincidental. Not only do you have the drive, ambition, and killer instinct like we discussed in Chapter 1, but you also have two guys who realized a long time ago that working was a losing proposition for them.

That does not mean neither of them did it- even Rockefeller worked long hours as a young man doing bookkeeping for $0.50 a day...he worked hard at it and enjoyed it. Just because working is a "losing proposition" doesn't mean if you are working you are a "loser". In order to graduate from working to working for the good of others (like employees), you have to know the value of hard work. You also must know it in a much deeper way than the stereotypical blue collar thoughts on the matter. Most rich people worked very hard at some point in their life. Silver spoon stories and royal fairy tales are very much the exception.

Bill Gates was programming himself early on...traffic counters for early computing. Steve Jobs collected Coke bottles for food money. Henry Ford serviced steam engines for Westinghouse. P. Nathan Thornberry laid tile, painted walls, cleaned apartments, delivered warranty policies, and repaired toilets.

Okay, so maybe that last guy isn't quite as significant (yet) as the prior three, but none of the above is a loser. All four had to experience the pain of survival and working to understand it, in order to give others the same opportunities and even improved opportunities over their own.

I am happy to report to you that not a single employee of mine has ever stayed awake for over 36 hours straight laying slate tile and grouting with an epoxy grout then sealing it all with three coats so it looked perfect for the client...and got paid nothing for it like I did.

As all of us look back on some of the really crazy levels of work we had to do, and the small amount of reward we received, we can't imagine ever getting anyone to work like we did for us- and we won't even make them try- but for everything we've done to this point we've now learned enough to graduate from working with muscles below the chin in every way possible.

Here is a reality you need to cope with directly as a home inspector, if in fact you are personally inspecting;

You cannot do it forever.

You have your strong points from Chapters 1 & 2. Now modify them to take anything you can that is "work" out of it. You are absolutely capping your income (and creating physical problems long term) every time you get in a crawl space or attic or climb on a roof. If you are still inspecting, you need to immediately bring on an assistant.

Train your assistant to place your ladders, remove electrical panel covers, inspect under vanities, check electrical outlets, and eventually examine roof coverings, attics, and foundations...leaving you free to accomplish more and do more good in the world. If in fact one of your strong points that you enjoy doing is inspecting, then inspect and investigate issues which are convenient and physically less taxing while putting together a report and communicating with your clients. It can even reduce your time on site, making your service more convenient for all involved.

Ideally, you don't work at all, but I'll split the difference with you for now and accept just taking the parts of the job which involve losing the use of your knees and potentially risking your life off the table. As soon as you are personally at 30 inspections per month, you cannot afford not to.

Oh, and if you happen to get on a roof today, keep in mind that you are likely farther off of a solid surface than those guys in the famous picture of Rockefeller Center's construction.

Chapter 8
The Customer is Never Right

Arguably the best role Samuel L. Jackson has ever played is the role of Jules Winnfield in Quentin Tarantino's film, "Pulp Fiction."

My favorite scene is the diner scene- when two robbers ("Pumpkin" and "Honey Bunny") decide they're going to hold the place up at gun point and take everyone's wallets and valuables…which Jules is happy to give into until one of them asks for his briefcase.

In this scene and this stretch of an analogy designed to bring into a home inspection book the movie Pulp Fiction, the customer was "Pumpkin" (who Jules quickly began referring to as "Ringo"), and what the customer wanted was everything valuable Jules had including his briefcase. The business owner in this analogy was Jules, and the fee for his services of handing over valuables was not being shot in the face over breakfast.

In wanting the briefcase, the customer was wrong. The customer wanted too much- and the consequences of getting too much would have likely been death for both Jules and the couple robbing him. They had no way of knowing this and just like in any transaction the business owner knew more about his product or service than the client. In a brilliant use of scripture, Ezekiel 25:17, and the help of two guns including his own and Vincent's to create a Mexican Standoff, the customer was given excellent service and exactly what he really wanted...walking out of that diner alive with more money than he came in with, without penalties relating to law enforcement involvement, and without injury.

This is of course an extreme example of the customer not knowing what he wants and being wrong, but it's exactly what a customer is- Pumpkin and Honey Bunny. Pumpkin thinks he knows what he wants, Honey Bunny is along for the ride and backing him up even if she really, really has to pee. The roles can be reversed of course, and sometimes only one of them shows up.

If a customer could actually hold a gun to your head to get what they thought they wanted without consequence, some of them would do so if that were the way the world worked. It would be your job as a business owner to take their gun just as Jules did, and deliver to them what they really wanted or needed.

This is one of those topics in which every one of us has been lied to almost since birth it seems. "The customer is always right" they say. They print it and post it on the wall at restaurants in the break room. They teach it in business school, and it's just wrong.

Here's the new way to say it:

"The customer is always to be made to feel as if they are right."

When you say "The customer is always right," it is inherently implied that the customer knows what they want, and this is not the case. If Henry Ford were to deliver what the customer wanted, he would have given them faster horses.

Before we started offering RecallChek, nobody was checking for recalls, and now over 75,000 homes are checked each month...and clients love it. Did they know you should be checking for recalls? No, because they had no idea what they wanted.

Whenever a business owner, inspector or non-inspector, starts a sentence with "my customers want to see..." and go on to describe some feature in their report or procedure they go through in their inspection, what they are really saying is, "If I were Jules in Pulp Fiction, I would be dead right now."

When a business owner lacks creativity or lacks the ability to put together products and services which are big sellers and profitable, they listen to the worst possible advice they could ever get, which comes from their current customers.

The problem with the practice of listening to those customers is that anyone can develop and implement exactly what consumers say they want, so the profitability for doing so is low. Additionally, the input you can actually receive in this regard is very minimal, usually consisting of a small portion of the people you know or clients you serve. Even that small amount of input is slanted based on how you were presenting an idea. Beyond that, your current client base already likes you, and you want to appeal to a whole new client base as well. If changing everything resulted in offending 100% of your clients and replacing them with five times as many clients that all paid better, it would be the right thing to do for your business.

Nobody told Steve Jobs that they wanted a "Trash Can" to drag and drop icons in on the first Macintosh. In fact, before the visual representation of icons existed no "customer" ever suggested it was something they wanted to my knowledge...and computers are utilized each and every day!

Home inspections are experienced by consumers approximately one time every seven years...and they forgot all about the last one if they're on their second or third. What they receive in the way of services, value added differentiators, and ultimately the report, is not something they will likely ever have any basis of comparison to, so even if you have a customer telling you how great you are...they are still not necessarily right. They have no earthly idea.

What does this mean for your home inspection business?

Immediately stop designing your home inspection reports, how you note defects, how you operate your business based on what the "customer" wants...because they don't know. Figure out what you have changed over the years that may be holding your business back, and other things you could change that could move your business forward in a meaningful way.

I'll give you one example- there are probably a hundred inspectors out there who carry tags to put on all the shut off valves in the home (water, gas, etc.). They print them up with branding and when they're at the inspection they will not only tie them to the valve, they will also note in their inspection report that they've done so, document the location, and insert a picture.

Their reason: My clients love it.

That is not a good enough reason to me. I need to see a real client benefit and a real benefit to my business in order for it to make a difference. I will often ask them the questions in this order:

1. Do your agents know you do it and do they use you because of it? *No.*

2. Do you get business because people see your name on the tag at the main water shut off behind the water heater? *No, not yet.*

3. Do your clients experience a real benefit? Has anyone ever called you and said their house was flooding and you saved them thousands because they knew where the valve was? *Oh yes, many times.* Really? How many times? *Well, once, but it might have happened other times!*

Maybe your responses are different, but the reality is this. Your product can make or break you. It can be too costly, it can take too long, it can be unappealing when it counts (when they're calling around to that "list of three.")

Identify three things you can diminish in your process which you have added (which you probably added for yourself more than anyone else), and then replace it with two things the client will really see and appreciate at the right time. Don't focus on cutting cost. Focus on cutting time and processes that make your model less than replicable.

Chapter 9
When In Doubt, Write a Check.

I find small claims court to be a therapeutic experience. You get to act like a lawyer for just a few minutes, and almost immediately you get the results of the proceedings.

I am happy to talk about my experience of being sued some 20+ times all in all. It doesn't really bother me. Half a dozen of the lawsuits had no merit and never saw a court room- they didn't come from clients or anyone we had any contractual relationship with at all- they came from competitors rattling sabers (followed by the sound of their tails between their legs.)

Out of all the others, almost every single one was a small claims court case where we prevailed in full or to a large extent, with one blatant exception- the Pelton Case.

The Pelton Case was a first for me for a few reasons. It was one of the larger small claims cases I had seen up to that point, it wasn't going to be settled and the Plaintiff was beyond unreasonable. The facts were so clearly on my side I couldn't possibly lose...or so I thought.

The background to this one is that we had a one year warranty (the kind we sell through real estate agents and are delivered to buyers at closing) with a homeowner by the name of Pelton. One day she called in a claim to us, which our average client does about once a year, and we dispatched a contractor. So far so good.

Her claim was that her furnace wasn't working. What we didn't know was that she had paid for one of those special "$79.00 Clean and Tune" offers she got in the mail and guess what...they told her she needed a new furnace in that brand new house she just moved into. What a surprise!

Of course, she neglected to mention any of this when she called, so we sent the contractor to her house and when he got there he called us. He said he could not test the furnace, because it was no longer installed. It is sitting in the driveway in pieces, and the homeowner has advised him that he doesn't need to get in the house at all, he just needs to look at the garbage in her driveway and tell us to send her a check.

We of course instructed him to leave and we informed her that if she wanted to have the furnace reinstalled, we would be happy to make whatever repairs were necessary under the terms and conditions of the policy. It literally says in four different places in the policy in large, bold lettering *"Call us first, unauthorized repairs will not be covered."*

She took her $5,000.00 furnace invoice to the Hamilton County Courthouse in Noblesville, Indiana and filed in small claims against us almost immediately.

Here's where it gets interesting.

After a claim against you exceeds a certain amount, usually around $1500.00 in most States, you have to have an attorney represent you in the proceedings if you are a corporation.

So I called our attorney, had him contact the court and notify them that we had representation. The first court date comes up, and he had another hearing that day...so it was postponed. Then we motioned for a continuance based on my schedule. We did that five or six more times, until eventually the judge scheduled a special session just for us on a Tuesday afternoon.

By the time I got there, the judge was already fuming. We had disrespected her courtroom, or so it had seemed to me at the time. Then my attorney started questioning the Plaintiff, then me, and it wasn't clear exactly what our case was. I tried to fix this when it was my turn to take the stand, but there was so much said up to that point that it was diluted.

Then I made a mistake...when the Plaintiff had time to question me as a witness, she just started telling her story all over again. I stopped her mid-sentence and said, "Is there a question somewhere in there?"

The judge immediately turned to me and said, "Mr. Thornberry, you are neither an attorney nor a judge in this courtroom, please allow the attorneys to make objections."

She then turned to the plaintiff and said, "Is there a question somewhere in there Ms. Pelton?" (I laughed a little inside at that point.)

Long story short, I did not get my story out well. I didn't get a chance to really hammer the Plaintiff with the contractual clauses she had clearly violated, nor did I get the chance to call into question the potentially unnecessary replacement which took place...we ended up splitting babies and I ended up paying $1500.00.

With attorney's cost, I ended up paying $2000.00+.

Now let's do some math. In just over 15 years of operating the business, literally tens of millions in revenue on the low end, I was sued just over 20 times. About half of those times it was small claims, and the worst one of those was a $5,000.00 complaint resulting in a $1500.00 judgment, which is the standing record.

Was it worth my time to go?

There was certainly some entertainment value. I'm not sure if I could have avoided every trip to court (some people just need to take you there to get it out of their system), but at the end of the day and after personally living through the experience, I can tell you it's not worth it. If I could go back in time, I would have made a reasonable settlement to every single one, even the ones where I was clearly right and prevailed in court.

In case you end up getting one of these small claims court summons with high enough damages being sought that you end up having to have an attorney present, I will give you the solution that worked well for me in every case after the Pelton case.

Simply hire the attorney to show up. That's it. Do not discuss the case with them prior. Do not spend any money with them beyond a single hour to show up, and I don't care if they are the worst attorney in town. All they have to do is stand up in court, say "I'm Bob the attorney, here on behalf of the corporation, and my client will handle the proceeding while I observe and advise," and then they sit down and shut up. Then you get the opportunity to make your case and speak intelligently about your profession, standards, and the very technical issue at hand. (There isn't an attorney in the world who understands home inspection like we do. Not one.) You will discover that the court will be much more receptive to your arguments when you're making them yourself and not hiding behind counsel in the informal setting small claims court provides.

Whether you're handling a lawsuit or a complaint (or a complaint that may turn into a lawsuit), take a step back and truly evaluate the value of your time and the relationships involved before making a determination as to what you should do. If someone is asking for money especially, it is really important it be handled properly...and you will notice I'm not suggesting that we are limiting your liability from a legal standpoint,

I'm in it to protect your profits.

Go now to www.RecallChek.com, log in, and go to the Resources section. At the very bottom you will find a "Complaint Form". Download it, review it, customize it for your own purposes, and save a copy on your laptop.

The next time you get a complaint, you will be prepared not only to handle the liability side of things, but also to evaluate the business side and make the right choice to maximize profit.

Chapter 10
What's In Your Bank Account
Doesn't Matter

On talk radio daily you will hear commercials for gold brokers. This book is anything but investment advice, but take it from me:

Gold is an indisputably terrible investment most all of the time.

Gold brokers will dazzle you with charts and graphs that compare the value of gold to the dollar, and their assessment that an ounce of gold bought a hundred years ago for $20.00 would be worth $1500.00 today is accurate, but let's compare that to one single company with a reasonable time period for investing- General Electric went from $1.00 in 1978 to around $25.00 today. Gold was at $208.00 an ounce in 1978, so one company that did "okay" is worth around 25 times as much as they were 35 years ago while gold is at around 7 times. Housing did better over the same time period at about 20 times...plus it was all financed so on the actual dollars spent adjusted for time funds were utilized, real estate was probably more like 40 to 50 times when it comes to return on investment.

The spikes you see in the value of gold are based only on paranoia, fear of currency instability, and great marketing in recent years from the gold brokers. Even with all that marketing and the boost it gets from news channels streaming live video of instability in the Middle East, the return on investment over the last 100 years has been terrible compared to other investments.

When you adjust the price of gold for inflation, you would have paid roughly $500.00 for an ounce of the stuff 100 years ago...and you'd have $1500.00 today. That is a terrible return on investment.

I'm sure some will disagree with me, and that's okay, most of them disagree for good reasons. They like the security of gold in the safe. They like knowing that if Armageddon happened tomorrow they would have real currency in their hands with which to purchase goods.

They would be better off building a bomb shelter and stocking it with supplies on which to live for twenty years.

I say this to draw the comparison not between gold and other investments, but rather between gold and cash. Gold is essentially like holding inflation-adjusted cash with a very minor growth in value. It is why the rich and successful in growth mode largely don't bother with it. They may use it to hedge inflation in their later years when they have established themselves as diversified and as low a risk portfolio as possible. I invest in metals when uncertainty takes the market for a roller coaster ride.

For now, as you're building your business you need to focus on that business as an asset more than any stock, metal, or hard asset. When it is built correctly, it spits out money very rapidly and almost automatically adjusts for inflation. With your direct involvement, it can be your fastest growing, highest performing investment and I'm not talking in terms of what consultants and coaches say about "investing in yourself"...I'm talking about a real investment.

Let's take a look at a real investment in your home inspection business which has a return unlike anything the stock market has ever seen...a single mailer, a follow up email, a follow up phone call, and one office visit. You can extrapolate the numbers however you wish, whether it be at 100 units or 10,000 units, the return is the same.

We did a test with The Elite Group in Southern California- the largest single location home inspection company in the history of the industry. They have three sales people full time as I write this book and by the time you read it maybe they'll have four or five. They're hitting offices at an alarming rate and doing 15,000+ inspections per year. At this point, it would be a safe assumption that every agent in the market knows who they are and if they were going to have given them a shot they would have by now, and that assumption would be wrong. We proved it by sending out 10,000 mailers, at an expense of around $1.50 per mailer. Here's what it consisted of:

1. A "Priority Express" envelope, inkjet printed with a plain name return address and the address of the agent. (Available from The Inspector Services Group)

2. Two tri-fold brochures, featuring USP's including RecallChek, SewerGard, and MoldSafe. (From www.UltimateInspectorBrochures.com)

3. A separate buck slip summarizing what the SewerGard and MoldSafe covered and how they

can benefit the buyer.

The advertisement piece also included a "Prices starting at only..." heading.

We'll just analyze 100 of those mailings for simplicity's sake, total cost at around $150.00. (If you only did 100 it would probably end up a little bit higher since there is an upfront cost for set up and you get a discount for printing in volume)

On approximately 100 mailers that went to agents within a 5 mile radius of the home of one of The Elite Group's sales people, 2 agents gave them new referrals including one that does several dozen transactions a year. This is from an office which never used them- but when the agents read about what The Elite Group offered and compared it to what they were getting from another provider, a couple of the agents decided to make the switch.

In this case The Elite Group is now netting 30+ inspections a year because of an approximate $150.00 investment along with an estimated $500.00 worth of follow-up work (one week of labor for a salesperson.) But let's say the results weren't so great. Let's say that instead of two agents they only got one, and instead of a super agent doing 30+ transactions a year let's say they did six.

If that agent stayed with them for three years, at six inspections, averaging $350.00 per inspection, the total gross billing on that account would come out to $6,300.00. In The Elite Group's model, that may mean a $1500.00 profit, less the initial cost of the mailing and the follow up marketing, so around $850.00 net.

$850.00 may not seem like much, but let's put that in perspective. They spent $650.00 getting to it, and the return was paid out over a period of three years. Not only is that a better return on investment than 99% of what you'll find on the stock market (and certainly better than metals, CD's, and bonds), but it's totally scalable. You can spend $6,500.00 getting a return of $8,500.00, $65,000.00 getting a return of $85,000.00, and so on and so forth.

There is a finite limit to where a mailing like this can take an inspection company, but we haven't reached it yet even in the case of The Elite Group who started off mailing out 10,000 pieces.

What's in The Elite Group's bank account doesn't matter. Do you think they would rather have $650.00 in the bank, or $1500.00 coming in monthly over 36 months? Let's change those numbers to $65,000.00 in the bank, or $150,000.00 coming in over the next 36 months? Obviously, the latter.

As you read this book, you may have less than $65,000.00 to invest in marketing, but that's a good thing. It forces you to make good decisions. Even if you have $65,000.00 to invest in marketing, operate like you have $10,000.00 and do a small test. Here's how you do it, and we'll use the example of the mailing since it has been proven to work.

Step 1

Develop a Target List

Comb the real estate magazines at the grocery store or call on a friend with access to the listing systems. Identify the top 500 agents in your market on both the buying and listing side, or as close to it as you can get. You may find the top 10 list has a few agents who specialize in investment properties or they are a BLB (Broad Listing Broker) for HUD properties or bank repos. Exclude those agents. Once you have your list together, put them into a spreadsheet with Name, Address, Website, Email, and Phone Number. Yes, this is a research intensive project, but it is well worth it.

Step 2

Develop the Ultimate Mailer

This may seem self-serving, and in some ways it is of course, but you need to make sure you add to your inspection business, at the very minimum, RecallChek and SewerGard for the purposes of having an effective mailer. I am not saying this because they are my products, I am saying it because they are the only products on the market which can give you the ability to say two things in your mailing that will stir interest and give you the best return on investment;

   a. *Free Repairs (on recalled items).*

   b. *If your client's sewer line fails, we'll dig up their yard and fix it.*

The free repairs gets them reading, the sewer line repairs stir an emotional response and gives you a definitive point of differentiation which most inspectors can't compete with. Every real estate office has a horror story floating around the office about a sewer line failure, and the agents feel helpless (and sometimes get named in a lawsuit) over this issue. The home inspectors don't check the lines typically, the home warranties don't cover them, and it's nearly impossible to throw the seller in the line of fire for liability because you can't prove they knew about the issue buried in the front yard.

When you put together the mailer, it needs four components.

1. An enticing package. We sell a "Priority Express" envelope that works incredibly well- it looks like you paid for overnight service but it ships with a regular stamp. There are other ways to accomplish making sure every one gets opened, for instance you could put it in a bubble mailer or something else 3-dimensional. Whatever you do make sure it can't be ignored as junk mail.

2. A short, two paragraph letter. Something personal that makes an immediate impact... "I'm the best for your clients because..."

3. Two or three killer brochures. Simple tri-folds, which focus on USP's and testimonials, printed on premium paper and professionally designed. Steal ideas from www.UltimateInspectorBrochures.com .

4. A two-sided "buck slip". If you folded a letter sized paper in three parts, and cut off one part, you'd have a "buck slip". It's a different size so it stands out, and then on one side you focus on free repairs from RecallChek and on the other side you focus on coverage offered through SewerGard. The small amount of space forces you to get to the point, which yields great results.

Step 3

Implement!

A successful implementation in this scenario would be doing a big enough test, in the best manner possible, that you can determine the return on investment. It doesn't matter whether you make money on the first go or not. It is more a matter of doing it, learning from it, and creating streams of revenue on an ongoing basis.

Several years ago I was working with a partner, and the budget issue came up. Up until that point, every company with whom I had ever worked evaluated an opportunity, looked at their budget, and determined what they were going to spend and for how long before they re-evaluated and determined whether it would be a part of the following year's budget. When I asked about the budget, I thought I knew what the client wanted and the best way to work with them.

I was wrong.

This is the response I got, and it changed my business forever:

"There are no budget limitations for something that works."

When I heard that, it was like I had been asleep at the wheel of my business for my entire career and I had just woken up. I got off that phone call, started evaluating things in my own business that were working, and I began investing in them heavily. What was in the bank account didn't matter anymore – it was about what systems could be created.

That client ended up spending literally millions with me, and is still sending me checks every single month. Around every six months we meet and determine how we can both make more money. We never use the "B" word (budget).

That is how business should be.

Chapter 11
Debt Doesn't Matter

The Dave Ramsey followers of the world have this concept that debt is bad, a concept that goes way back and is even mentioned in scripture that some use to justify their position on debt.

There are a number of false beliefs floating around and being promoted about what the Bible says when it comes to debt. Some say that it's a sin to borrow, while others say it is wise to borrow. Some say it's a sin to loan money, while some say things like "debt is an exercise in faith" and "God will bail you out of debt".

All of these statements are untrue of course, but even if they were, the modern concept of debt was not the norm in Biblical times.

All the same, whether you subscribe to The Bible, The Koran, the Bhagavad Gita, or no religious text at all, we all subscribe to basic human values and being enslaved by debt flies in the face of our independent spirit.

This rings especially true for business owners.

We not only have our homes and the future of our kids on the line, we have the homes and futures of the all the kids that work for all of our employees on the line.

Using debt responsibly is assumed when I say "debt doesn't matter." I'm not giving you a license to go mortgage your home to 120% of its value, open up department store credit cards at will, and rack up six figures in credit card debt on lavish vacations.

What I am giving you license to do is take on responsible debt, especially the kind where the obligation from the lender is just as important as the obligation from you to the lender.

Sometimes debt puts you in the position of control, and oftentimes it can force accountability through underwriting. When you need money, whether it is to buy another vehicle, purchase an office building, or finance an acquisition, it is the responsibility of the lending institution to not only have the money available to lend to you and determine if you are creditworthy to protect their assets, it's also their responsibility to vet the deal and give insight.

In other words, if you go to the bank with a really crappy plan, they should turn down the loan and they just did you a favor. I've been the recipient of that favor a few times, especially in my younger years.

On the other hand, if they extend you credit, it means they see it as very likely that you will pay back the loan in full and gain a benefit that you wouldn't have been able to attain on the cash you had available. It's a win-win.

Most home inspectors will never have the need to talk to a business banker in reality. They will at most open up an account that they could do at the teller window and maybe get a credit card that they could have applied for online.

That's not good enough for you.

You need to go to your local bank and create a relationship with a V.P. or above. They'll even buy you lunch, and that's not a joke.

Additionally, you need to make sure your business is an S-Corp. LLC's are fine, and definitely serve most of the same purposes, but the way they are looked upon by the bankers (and by the public) is much better.

Many of these branch V.P.'s aren't MBA grads, most

have never owned their own business, and many of them are very young. They have quotas to fill, and you want to be a part of that.

On every form they see every day, there are three choices for business types: Sole Proprietorship, LLC, and Corporation.

Most of these forms don't even make a distinction between S-Corp and C-Corp. The only thing most bank V.P.'s know about LLC's is that you can pay $49.00 for one according to that LegalZoom commercial and that the first two letters stand for "Limited Liability." The only thing they know about Corporations is that all of their biggest clients seem to own one.

Here are your goals with the banker. First, you need to establish the kind of relationship where if he knows someone who you can help or if he knows someone that could help your business, that he will pick up the phone. He thrives on being a connector. Second, you need to make sure you have one account there (while maintaining accounts elsewhere too), as well as financing all of your vehicles through him. Third, you need to establish a credit line with him, and let him be your guide on how to do it. The credit line should be for $50,000.00.

After you get this done, even if you only finance one vehicle and open up a credit line that you don't have a use for, your ability to get things done will be improved greatly. Put a couple thousand bucks on the credit line and pay the payment every month just to make sure they keep it open and never put it under review. It's a small price to pay to have $48,000.00 available and a guy you can call to prepare a certified check to buy your next vehicle without even filling out an application.

Your goal in all of this is to have greater abilities than the competition, and it is surprisingly easy to achieve this. It may not happen in a day or even a week, but everything I've described here can happen in a matter of months even if your credit isn't great.

The picture at the front of this chapter is a Federal Courthouse. That's where you go to file bankruptcy, and if your Corporation is set up correctly it won't sting too badly. Milton Hershey, Walt Disney, H.J. Heinz, P.T. Barnum, Henry Ford, Abraham Lincoln, and even Nathan Thornberry have all been there. Coincidentally, all of the above had great ambitions prior to claiming bankruptcy for one or more corporations or personally, all of the above regretted having to do it, and after the bankruptcy all of the above were a great deal more successful...which kind of flies in the face of the Biblical arguments regarding debt.

Chapter 12
No Excuses

Right before I wrote this chapter I sent an email to 10,000 home inspectors, all of whom we either met at shows or already work with actively as users of RecallChek, 90-Day Warranties, SewerGard, etc. It had a simple offer in it:

"I'll pay the first 400 inspectors who want it $105.00 to watch the 4 DVD set of our inaugural Power User Conference (2013)."

Of course the offer had terms and conditions, the first being you need to pay us $395.00, but in exchange you get $500.00 in lab fees from InspectorLab, so you come out ahead by $105.00 in services you'll probably use anyways plus you get the DVD set.

It may seem like a no-brainer to you and I. I set it up that way.

What should have happened is that I would lose $42,000.00 immediately in lab fees alone, another $4000.00 in postage, another $1600.00 in DVD printing, and of course the actual cost of producing the DVD with our staff of video production experts, but discounting that cost we are at a loss of $47,600.00.

We had a lot of debate around the office over how we offer the video of our conference. There were staff members who thought we should never release it, others that thought we should only offer it to those who actually attended, some who thought we should offer it to inspectors who attend the following year, and a few that thought we should offer it for $1000.00 to clients only.

After all, the value of the DVD alone is immense. If you wanted to see the event live, you would have to pay $300.00-$500.00 for the ticket, $400.00 for the hotel room, plus around $400.00 for the flight, all in all around $1300.00. Plus the event is exclusively for clients, so even being invited requires spending some amount of money.

We made the offer anyways, almost as an experiment. Here is an event where around 200 of the largest inspection companies in the world come for marketing advice- and you get all 10 hours of it to watch in your home at your convenience and we even pay you $105.00 to watch the thing.

The results were as follows:

1. We did not hit the 400 orders in the first day. It took over two weeks.

2. Over 15% of the orders cancelled once we asked for payment (and almost all of them were non-clients).

3. Over 80% of the orders were from clients.

4. Most of the attendees of the conference on the DVD purchased the DVD.

If you're keeping up with the math, the experiment had almost the exact results our staff had hoped for initially. Around 5% of the DVD's delivered were to non-clients. Most of the DVD's went to attendees of the event, and the rest went to current clients.

So basically I spent $47,600.00 delivering my own clients a DVD. I consider it money well spent. Just like it will cost money for me to get this book into the hands of my clients (and it is exclusively for our clients, I do not want to train non-clients to compete with you), the DVD did as well. I am okay with that because those clients that watch the DVD, read this book, go to the Power User Conference...they grow their businesses. Since our growth is dependent on the growth of our clients, these expenditures are investments, and they have been the best investments we have ever made.

There were a couple of inspectors who shifted their mindset as a result of the offer. Two inspectors that ordered the DVD immediately sent me an email to cancel and told me they did not offer mold testing and made a mistake.

I asked both why they did not, and both had similar responses indicating their clients didn't ask them for it.

My response to them was that nobody was ordering Cappuccinos from McDonald's until they opened McCafe, and now it is the reason McDonald's is hitting record numbers.

Neither ended up buying the DVD, but both are now offering mold testing. It just took the right catalyst, which in this case was the McCafe argument, to get them to stop making excuses.

You and I both make excuses for not doing something that would be good for our business, and both of us need to stop doing that! We make up all sorts of excuses, don't we? Some of the time we look at the numbers and cannot justify spending the money, other times we think we can do something better ourselves, whatever the excuse is it's nothing more than an excuse. There are companies doing millions and others doing billions in revenue that have already figured it out...why do we resist taking their lead?

In the case of these two inspectors, I had to virtually give them a pump and some Air-O-Cells to get them to offer a service that literally every inspection company doing seven figures in the history of home inspection offers. You might read that story and feel sorry for them.

I wonder if there is a CEO somewhere looking at my decisions in the same way.

Let me give you an example of a very difficult decision I had to make recently to put something in place that literally every company doing a billion in sales has...and yet I made excuse after excuse before finally giving in.

Last year I decided it was my last year at the helm of Residential Warranty Services and The Inspector Services Group. The value of me running the day to day operations paled in comparison to developing new products, acquiring other businesses, and doing high level marketing projects like a new web development platform we will launch in 2015 or writing this book. So I hired a headhunter at no small fee to find a Director of Operations, and subsequently hired a Director of Operations at no small expense. The most qualified I could find.

This is where my excuses, the things keeping me from achieving, start showing themselves.

The first thing the new Director does is establish that we need to do some construction in the office to reduce noise in our call centers.

There's a few thousand bucks gone, but no big deal. I do not even review the thing- I take my own advice from Chapter 3 and I get out of the way. So far so good.

Then he identifies inefficiencies in how we handle phone calls, and the potential for long term savings on phone service that currently runs us around $50,000.00 per year. (Yes, that is our current phone bill just for landlines as I write this book)

Perhaps foolishly, I am still in the loop when it comes

to capital expenditures, so the tens of thousands of dollars we will be spending on new phone equipment and upgrades to wiring throughout our facilities in Indy, Fort Lauderdale, and two other locations in the U.S. lands on my desk for approval.

There goes a few tens of thousands, a little more heartburn, but the long-term savings making it an investment I can live with. Approved.

Then comes the real panic moment for me as a business owner.

My Director of Operations comes to me with something we need. More specifically, a person we need. "We need an HR director," he tells me.

That is not an easy pill to swallow.

It is one of those moments when you have to think about all those 9600 inspectors who received an email saying, "Here's a DVD of something the leading inspection companies in the country, people who make many times over what you do, for you to watch and benefit from, and I'm actually going to pay you to watch it," and you start seeing parallels between their terrible decision-making over a few hundred bucks and wonder if you are doing the exact same thing over a few thousand bucks a month.

Big companies not only have HR directors, they have entire departments. My neighbor of 10 years was the HR director for a major jet engine manufacturer, and I think back to the first conversation I ever had with him about his occupation. I remember thinking how ridiculous it was that a corporation would pay that guy obscene money not to recruit, not to do performance reviews, not to actually make the company any money directly. His job, as he described it, was basically to make sure every employee at his company had the best benefits, he made sure the company was held accountable in delivering those benefits, and that raises and vacations were implemented. He even made sure birthdays were remembered and anniversaries of employment were recognized with gold watches and plaques.

I did not get it. Now I do to some extent. It is all about talent retention and saving money on training and recruiting. Employees should be talking about their jobs when they go home and when they are out with friends. Everyone in town should want to work for your exciting company. It is what every Fortune 500 company has, which makes it indisputable that if you are at the point of needing an HR person and being able to afford one and you do not...you are a fool.

So I get out of the way, and just do what every other CEO does- take a perfectly round ice cube, put it in a glass, and pour the most expensive old scotch I can find in my bar over it slowly and try to forget the many hundreds of thousands of dollars that were just spent. Later I laugh about paying one guy thousands to find me another guy to pay a bunch of money to so that he can tell me to hire a HR director that I can pay a bunch of money to in order to make sure that we spend a bunch of money on our employees. Read that one twice and tell me you're not looking for a scotch yourself!

All of us have our threshold for what we are willing to make excuses for. If you are reading this book I hope you are beyond making excuses over a few hundred dollar one time purchase. Most inspectors in my top 1,000 list are at the low end not being quite sure about spending $3.00-$4.00 per inspection with ISN, in the middle not being totally comfortably with spending

$500.00 a week on a marketing person, to at the high end getting nervous over $100,000.00 cash outlays for acquisitions or offering higher salaries for lead inspectors or business managers.

The more you can do without making excuses, the farther you will go, and the farther you go the less you will be making excuses. Did the chicken or the egg come first? I have no idea, but in this case dropping the excuses has to come first to some extent, at least to the limit of your ability to maintain the improvements you make for the short period of time it takes for them to have positive results.

Here is a plan you need to drop the excuses and just do, for two reasons:

1. *The cost can be contained and the results measured.*

2. *Literally all of the $1 million + home inspection operations in the U.S. and Canada have implemented the same things in all or in part.*

Just be glad you are not going to have to spend the money on an HR director anytime soon. These decisions are easy, and I have broken them down into

26 steps. Just like I do not need anyone to justify why an HR director is right for my business because literally every company that is creating the revenue levels I want to create has one, you do not need to justify anything here either because when you look at the home inspectors making the most money, they have implemented most or all of the list.

Pretend you hired me as the General Manager or Director of Operations at your home inspection company and I gave you this list of things and told you this is what we need to do to get to $1 million in sales. My resume included working in the home inspection industry literally all my life, growing up in a multi-inspector firm that does millions, and consulting/serving over 80% of the $1 million + companies throughout the U.S. and Canada.

That is my real resume. Now here is the list;

A. Ensure 10-20 real estate offices are delivered brochures each and every business day. If this requires the hiring of a marketing rep, so be it.

B. Get updated brochures (a minimum of 5,000) and materials from

www.UltimateInspectorBrochures.com or
another reputable source, professionally
designed, with the following Unique Selling
Propositions included;

    a. RecallChek

    b. SewerGard

    c. 90-Day Warranties

    d. Offerings including Mold Testing, Pool &
       Spa Inspections

    e. Money Back Guarantee

C. Get the Power User Conference DVD's from
Inspector Services Group, and have key
personnel (Marketing and Administrative Only)
watch it.

D. Have the same key Personnel read The Hungry
Home Inspector.

E. Join the local REALTOR board(s) as an affiliate
member. Establish whatever relationship
necessary to gain electronic lockbox access.

F. Hire/Outsource Call Center Operations for

booking inspections with extended hours.

G. Implement Mold Testing immediately as a menu item.

H. Add a summary page to Inspection Reports and ensure the rest of the report is done by system.

I. Ensure same day delivery of reports.

J. Establish banking relationship (as described in Chapter 11).

K. Establish a regular mailing campaign (like the one described in Chapter 10).

L. Hire inspectors (or assistants) as soon as the level of 30 inspections per month is established.

M. Implement ISN (Inspection Support Network) immediately.

N. Implement the RecallChek App immediately (using the ISN integration).

O. Add videos for the Buyer's and Seller's confirmation emails (like the ones found at www.InspectorServicesGroup.com)

P. Get booth materials from www.UltimateInspectorMarketing.com and set up a booth at local and regional REALTOR events.

Q. Implement the BAM Dashboard for sales efforts at www.BAMdashboard.com .

R. Book ticket for business owner and marketing/office manager for the Power User Conference at www.PowerUserConference.com and get on a regular CE program for all inspectors (company provided).

S. Get quotes once annually for E & O Insurance from Allen Insurance, InspectorPro, and others to compare rates continuously. Get suggestions from ISG since they cover E & O Deductibles and work with insurers in their claims processes.

T. Automatically populate RecallTrak data for referring agents.

U. Schedule a minimum of 1 sales presentation monthly.

V. Establish company as a S-Corp.

W. Create multiple websites, focusing on different

areas and specialties. Outsource the web development.

X. Log into www.HomeInspectionForum.net , register, establish a signature line with links to your web page, and post at least once a week.

Y. Call around to a minimum of 5 competitors per month and get pricing and offering data to ensure you stay ahead of the competition.

Z. Get branded shirts and have logos installed on vehicles.

That is the short list. If you get through all of them, you will absolutely be doing anything and everything that every one of the most successful inspection companies in the country does. When you add up the cost it is minimal. Maybe a few thousand dollars is all it takes to be the biggest and the best. You do it, you will be wildly successful, and not everyone will be your biggest fan. The next chapter is all about coping with the consequences of your success!

Before we go on, let's talk about the list for a moment. A-Z. That is 26 items. Not one of them is particularly offensive, I am not suggesting in any of them to do something ethically challenging, so why is it that there is a very high likelihood that we will not have 100% of the readers of this book doing 100% of the line items above?

Excuses.

How do we get rid of excuses?

The only objection I can possibly imagine to the list above being a real concern would be budget. Let's say the cash outlay is $1000.00 to get half the list done.

I will let you in on a little secret. We only printed 2,000 copies of this book and we have kept records of exactly who received it. If 2,000 inspectors make their way through half of the list above, the effect on their businesses will be enormous, and since you have read this far I will extend you the credit. At least a few of those items will be from The Inspector Services Group, and I am confident you can get through half of this list on $1000.00...I will finance that. For all 2,000 recipients of this book. No interest, other than the interest I have in your success.

If there are any other excuses let me know. If I told my Director of Operations, who gives me more like 20 action items a month he will be spending (my) money on, "no" on a regular basis, he would just quit. I hired him because of his resume, his ability to make decisions, and to run very large-scale operations, and if he did not see a commitment from the ownership to growth, the opportunity for growth wouldn't be as great.

Chapter 13
Success Has Consequences

Ending a book on Chapter 13 (excluding the Resources chapter) might seem like a bad idea if you are superstitious, but I am not. I know bad things are going to happen, regardless of how many ladders you avoid walking under today or how hard you try to make sure everything goes smoothly.

You will get sued at some point if you are doing a million in sales. Probably multiple times.

Competitors and even some agents will talk badly about you. In *The Hungry Home Inspector* I made mention of a webinar I was doing when a home inspector from the East Coast started bad mouthing The Elite Group (which is on the West Coast), even though he had no direct knowledge of their business at all.

Why does this happen? In a word, hate.

It is basic human nature to hate, and since the beginning of time humans have been attacking, murdering, and even enslaving other humans for whatever reason is in vogue at the time. Race and religion seem to be the most common historically and are making headlines in many parts of the world right now to this day.

In the U.S., Canada, and other countries around the world not involved in religious and territorial conflicts, the reasons for hate are different and luckily so are the results. We are no longer having witch trials in Salem.

There have been studies to back up all of the following reasons why someone might hate you, many of which seem obvious but others more subtle. Some reasons for hate seem just ridiculous.

One reason people might hate you would be that you have a wide face. Men with wide faces are perceived to be more aggressive and dishonest.

Growing a beard can also land you in the crosshairs of being hated. Sure, they are gaining in popularity once again, and maybe you look better and feel more confident knowing you can get on a snow mobile with less risk of frostbite, but people associate beards with aggression and the majority of people believe you are more likely to be a criminal if you have one.

If you think those are weird reasons to be hated, try

this one: Giving people compliments.

Giving a compliment is a minefield. If you are a salesperson and you compliment a prospect, even if they believe you are sincere, their guard goes up. Even if you are not in sales and you compliment someone, they may receive it well...but the person standing next to them gets jealous.

If you are really into science, you are seen as socially awkward. Sorry.

If you are passionate about a cause, maybe it is environmentalism, feminism, or political causes like conservatism or liberalism...anyone not in your camp will hate you for it on some level.

Posting a "selfie" on Facebook every day while you're doing relatively unexciting things can get you in hot water with people...especially the kind of people who see all of your posts because they are at home all day on Facebook.

Sweating, not from exercise but rather from stress, will emit an odor that makes people naturally not want to be around you...yes, you can even smell desperation and have people itching to get away from you.

Feeling lonely and depressed definitely will not win you any popularity contests, which brings us to the top 2 reasons for being hated in our modern society according to P. Nathan Thornberry:

Atheism and Success.

Studies have shown over and over again that people- even non-religious people- distrust atheists. There have been studies done where respondents, when asked who would be most likely to take money from a wallet they found, more often picked "atheist" than "rapist". I am not kidding. People trust atheists less than people who have the defining characteristic of sexually assaulting other people.

That is pretty strong hate, but it pales in comparison to the top spot on the list- Success.

Life is graded on a curve, and by definition your success means that others are less successful. You will find yourself to be under greater scrutiny, constant attacks, and you will even find that others will conspire against you.

There was a wildly successful startup in the early 2000's in Indianapolis called "HomeYeah!", and they had a great model. You list your home with them, get limited advice, but your home gets into the MLS rather than being a For Sale By Owner that no one sees. The fee was a flat fee of around $900.00 if I recall correctly.

HomeYeah! read the rules and regulations, both from a licensing perspective and the MLS rules, and they operated within the confines of it.

The agent who was the "Listing Agent" on HomeYeah! listings ended up being the #1 listing agent by volume in Central Indiana...after only a few years in business.

That is when things started heating up for HomeYeah!.

Over the two years following their best year, one of the largest brokerages in town started targeting their listings hard. They even had a closet full of HomeYeah! signs. They made bashing their company virtually a part of their listing presentations.

Another broker sitting on the board at the professional licensing agency went to work on the rules to try to make their lives more difficult. Brokers at the local Board of REALTORS did the same with the MLS rules.

Two years after their biggest year ever, their business model was toast. No longer could you simply hand a client forms and put their home in the MLS. Now you had to meet with them, go through the listing agreement, and actually be at the closing. Essentially, the competition regulated that full-service real estate was the only option.

Success created not just hate, but outrage from the rest of the real estate community. At their rate of growth, they might have had offices in 30 states by now and would be a large company.

What they should have done was started off with more than one listing agent. That was their first mistake. When you are driving down the street, you only see so many real estate signs. Each individual agent and broker in the marketplace would not have been so overwhelmed and threatened by their numbers if they did not show up as the #1 listing agent every single week in their MLS. It was an embarrassment for the large brokerages with rock star $50 million + agents who were used to being on top. Being the number one listing broker was not a marketing edge for HomeYeah!, so there wouldn't be any negative consequences in their business for splitting up listings other than a few hundred bucks in membership dues and perhaps a slight drop in efficiency. I have a feeling that insiders at the local Board of REALTORS did not like their business model either. How many small-time dues paying agents were not on their membership list because of this one single listing juggernaut?

The second thing they should have done is gotten slightly more involved in the transactions, and offered more optional services for additional fees. One of the realities of showing a listing of theirs and writing an offer is that the buyer's agent was basically dealing with a for sale by owner, and only getting paid for one side. With just a small amount of advising for their clients, the agents showing their listings would not have been made to feel like they were doing double the work for half the money.

The third thing they should have done is volunteered for board positions and gotten involved in the MLS rules quietly. Those positions are not paid, not a lot of people want to do them, so it would have been easy to sneak in and have a seat at the table.

The fourth and final thing they should have done, if the new regulations were being proposed anyway, is take legal action. It would have been a bit of money, but sometimes that is the investment you need to make in your business. They would have been well served to name every single one of the brokers personally who sat on the boards making these new rules, that were indisputably designed to put a stop to their business model, in an antitrust case.

Before I go any further with this legal strategy, I want to be clear that I am talking about what HomeYeah! should have done for their own business, which isn't to say that I do not personally see the benefits to full-service real estate. There were many transactions I saw where the clients in this limited service model were not getting a great deal. Sometimes they priced too low and left money on the table. Other times the listings were priced too high and a family who needed to sell their home were stuck with a perpetual listing that spent too long on the market. The brokers who pushed for the rules that demolished the limited service business model probably thought they were doing great things for the industry and maybe even believed they were doing good for consumers, for the reasons I have outlined.

All the same, the leadership at HomeYeah! failed to act and if they had sued under antitrust laws, they could have done it in such a way where they would not actually have to go to court to maintain their business model.

Many of these boards are simply made up of business owners (brokers in this case) and not attorneys. They probably did not know they had some exposure when it came to antitrust laws, or if they did they pushed forward knowing they were taking a calculated risk. Most of these boards also have insurance policies protecting directors and board members, and that is where the legal strategy gets interesting.

If the brokers had been named personally, it is very likely that they would have to give notice to their insurer. The insurer would step in to defend the case, but before they started spending legal funds mounting a defense, they would first take a look at the issue and meet with the board. Meanwhile HomeYeah! could have filed for a temporary injunction to prevent changes to the rules while the legal issues were sorted out, which they would almost certainly have been granted.

When the insurance company's attorneys looked at the issue, they would have immediately identified the protectionism aspect of the issue and reported back to the insurance company that the case would go away without having to spend another dime if the board would simply not move forward with changing these rules to eradicate the limited service model. They would advise the board of this as well.

At that point, the insurance company would have been in the driver's seat, and they have no interest in the issue that these brokers were so passionate about. They have an interest in not spending tens of thousands or even hundreds of thousands of dollars defending the case.

When the significant others of the brokers involved started getting certified letters and even Sheriff's service at their homes, the pressure would have been on to resolve the issue from the personal side as well.

Now the landscape changes completely. No attorney I have ever met is willing to suggest that a case is a slam dunk, because anything can happen in a courtroom.

The insurer may even tell the board that if they want to continue down the path, that the insurer will not be responsible for their defense and cancel their policy. After all, they did not write them a policy which gave them license to act unlawfully.

Once the board members are advised that they could lose, they have been advised that they themselves or the board will have to spend the money to defend the case, and the pressure from home is mounting, the issue may go away.

If it does not, then you decide how far to press the issue and what to spend on it. At the end of the day, the other side has to have something to lose in order for you to have any chance at getting your way.

In your home inspection business, you very well may experience something similar. In licensed states, board positions are disproportionately held by low-volume inspectors who have all day to work as an unpaid consultant to the state to tell you how to run your business. If they see you as a threat, you may have to contend with a similar issue to what HomeYeah! did, and you may have to take similar actions to what I suggested they should have done.

When you are doing a lot of volume, and walking the thin line we walk in the home inspection industry, you are going to cause a problem for someone at some point. It may result in losing an agent, or perhaps even an entire office not referring you for a period of time. It will happen, how you deal with it is what makes the difference.

When you find yourself hated in an office, the first thing you need to do is back off. Take a couple weeks off from marketing in that office. Find an insider or two who are friendly to you and sympathize with your situation, and gather intelligence.

Let the situation simmer down. If the angst subsides, show up again and everyone will forget the problems from last month when they experience the successes of this month. I promise you that every agent in that office has much better things to do with his time than focus on hating you...unless he is in the mood to hate you and you come barging in the door.

If the problem does not go away quickly, it is usually a

particular agent who is making all the noise. Let it happen for a few months- the longer it goes the crazier they seem. Market quietly and get a few agents to use you, and at some point the crazy person will make a statement and two or three very reasonable people will back you up, letting everyone know that crazy people do not like you, reasonable people do, so it would be crazy not to use you. It is the best advertising you can possibly get.

In fact, finding yourself at the center of controversy can be great for business. Just like people sitting at home watching your Facebook posts get jealous easily and board members tend to not be the most active marketers, participants in online message boards like InterNACHI's tend to be equally crazy. To this day, there are a dozen "inspectors" on that forum talking about me all day long, and every time they do it is great exposure. The best salesperson I could possibly hire would be a crazy person who does not like me, and the same will work for you in a real estate office.

Hate towards you as a business owner can have a negative toll mentally if you allow it to, but the financial results are usually positive if you play the game correctly. If you are faced with a rule change, you know what to do. If you have a crazy person bad mouthing you, ignoring them while their rhetoric only increases in volume and frequency destroys their credibility and enhances yours. If you have competition that does not like you, and they want to spend their time at a chapter meeting talking about you, all the better. The more time they spend on you, the less time they have to actually compete.

The last form hatred can take is a lawsuit against you. Lawsuits can get nasty and they can be expensive. The money is not actually the stressful part, it is the negativity associated with being sued and the emotions you experience when spending the money.

I have been sued a few times, and I can tell you with absolute certainty that a year after a lawsuit ends, you will not remember what you spent on it and you won't care about the money side- you will only know what the effect was on your business. Try to remember this when you are in the middle of the case, it will help you make better decisions.

Lawsuits are not simple things to contend with, and there is no way I could possibly address every scenario in this book, so I will instead tell you to deal with lawsuits the same way you should deal with everything in your business if you are going to go big:

With strategy in mind.

Start with the end in mind. If you prevail, what is the result? How will others related to the issue see you? If you lose, what is the result? How will it affect your business? If you settle, what terms would best benefit you?

You cannot let anyone's input sway you from your strategy and looking at the return on investment. Legal professionals are good at legal stuff, but generally not good business advisers. The advice they give is solely designed to minimize your downside risk, but they do not know what the upside potential might be after the lawsuit is over. There are certain things they cannot do of course, mostly related to ethics, but when it comes to the strategy you want to pursue you tell them what it is, and advise them to minimize your downside risk within the confines of your chosen strategy.

When you deploy every strategy in this book, you will absolutely have a machine built for $1 million or more in sales annually. I don't have a single product or service which does less than seven figures a year after launch, and the first time I hit the million mark I was just out of high school- and this book basically went through every aspect of how I did it each time. The strategies work, but you do not have to use them. You can take bits and pieces, and create what you want to- whether that be a $1 million + home inspection firm, a very manageable quarter million dollar firm with just a few associates, or a premium single-man operation.

Join the conversation at www.homeinspectionforum.net and I'll see you at the next Power User Conference!

Chapter 14
Resources

Building a home inspection firm is remarkably easy from a cash requirement perspective. You can have all the best tools & resources with a small investment of time and less than $10,000.00 in cash. Here are a few of the necessities mentioned in this book that you will need to build your machine.

THE TRUTH

If a manufacturer has designed a dangerous product, they MUST recall all those items, and FIX THEM FOR FREE!

THE CATCH

It's up to the consumer to find out for themselves, which means searching through over 200 million recalled items online.

MAKE MORE MONEY
ON EVERY INSPECTION, IN
LESS THAN FIVE MINUTES.

Go Online & Sign Up Today!
www.RecallChek.com

Whether you are in the title, mortgage, or home inspection business; whether you are a single-man operation or have hundreds of sales reps, this system will help you grow your real estate referrals!

Track every marketing effort, automate your email marketing, log every phone call, and have your staff clock in on one easy to use web application that works well on both PC and Mac as well as mobile devices. More than 450 real estate vendors already utilize the Broker Agent Marketing Dashboard; and you can too with our free 90-Day Trial.

Your clients want more than just a home inspection, they need professionals they can depend on even after the job is done. Back all of your inspections with a 90-Day Structural and Mechanical Buyer's Home Warranty and give your clients peace of mind.

Grow Your Business Today!

800-544-8156

www.90daywarranty.com

This is a Home Inspection Business Owner Conference

Pure marketing and business implementation. If you're looking to grow your business, you can't afford to miss this event.

800-544-8156
www.poweruserconference.com